NO SHAME IN MY PAIN

FROM HOPELESSNESS TO WHOLENESS

Written By: Sierrah M. Chavis M.Ed

ISBN: 978-0-578-88367-0

Printed by Power Of Purpose Publishing
www.PopPublishing.com
Atlanta, Ga. 30326

I am dedicating this book to first, my mother who has been my biggest inspiration and push in life and who has shaped me into the person I am today. She has given up so much so that I can find my purpose and live in my truth and best version of myself. Thank you for never giving up on me and for always believing in me. I also dedicate this book to my daughters, Honure, Gracie, and Reign, and to empower you to know that life may be tough but so are you! You're more than enough and worthy of so much more! Mommy will always be there for you! I also dedicate this book to my aunt Renata aka "Flawless" thank you for always supporting me and for being my #1 Cheerleader through all of my accomplishments. Lastly, I dedicate this book to my husband for loving me unconditionally, for pushing me to tell my story, and not be ashamed of my past. Thank you for showing me what love should feel and look like each and every day and for restoring my hope in love again.

To those that read this book, may it transform and inspire you to be free of those painful things from your past that try to hold you back, from being your true authentic self. Have "No Shame in your Pain" and walk in your truth and purpose!!

Description:

"No Shame in my Pain" is about not being ashamed of the things in your life that have caused you trauma, hurt, and grief but to stand in front of your pain, acknowledge it and own it so you can begin to heal from it. This self-help book and journal takes you through the life story of some of the author's most painful moments in her life that she had to overcome, such as domestic violence, teen dating violence, miscarriage, cancer, and painful memories. The book walks you through defining self-love and turning your mess into a message and your test into a testimony. It's about living life without regrets and understanding that your pain matters. This book includes reflections to help you start to think about your own story, scriptures, quotes, and affirmations. It's time to heal, and the only way to heal is to deal with what is hurting you and give yourself permission to heal in time. There is no time limit as to how long it takes you to heal, but you should see growth throughout your healing journey and embrace the small victories that happen. Learn from your past but don't allow it to define your future.

The Hopelessness focuses on the *Pain,* while Wholeness focuses on the *Healing* journey.

Contents

Contents

HOPELESSNESS

There is no greater agony than bearing an
untold story inside of you.
~Maya Angelou ~

Chapter 1: Abandoned

My pain started as a little girl. I had abandonment issues from my biological father. At the age of four, I remember waiting on the steps of my grandparent's home for my father, who had promised that he would pick me up. I remember being so excited and getting dressed up in my pretty dress and fancy shoes; I would wait for hours until the sun went down. My mom would come out and sit next to me and say, "it's time to come back inside the house, baby." I can remember asking my mom why? She would look into my eyes filled with water; Grabbing my hand and saying to me, "something came up, baby, but don't worry, he will come next time." My mom tried her best to protect me from being hurt. She would make up stories to me about the reason he didn't come. I felt empty on the inside, foolish and abandoned. Why didn't my father want me? What was wrong with me? My mom would eventually marry, and he took me under his wing and loved me like I was his own. I would call him dad because he protected me, loved me, and provided for me, as a father should for their child. Although he was a great man, I still, deep down, suffered from abandonment issues from my biological father. As I got older, those feelings didn't go away. I remember being in middle school, and my step-dad wanted to adopt me, and my mom and step-dad came to me asking how I would feel about him adopting me. I was happy because all I ever wanted was to feel loved, but a part of me wanted my biological father to love me too. When I found out that without hesitation, my biological father signed over his parental rights, I felt unwanted and unloved. The feeling that I had of abandonment from him hurt so bad. I didn't know how to feel and would become numb thinking about it. I eventually had to release this pain, but it wasn't easy. I had to be honest with myself about where this feeling of wanting to be loved and accepted was coming from? By accepting that I had some real issues of feeling unloved and unaccepted by my biological father, it helped me to heal. I eventually had to confront my father about these issues that I suffered with as a child. Did it fix anything? No, but what it did for me was to release that pain and no longer be a prisoner of the mind. I could express my feelings and thoughts; although it didn't fix or change anything, it did allow me to be free. It allowed the weight to be lifted, and I was able to begin my healing. Part of the healing journey that I found to help me was to stop blaming myself for someone else's problems. I can't change people, but I can change how I deal and heal.

Have you ever dealt with abandonment?

What are some specific things that have made you feel unwanted?

What are some ways that you can confront those fears of abandonment?

_____

_____

_____

_____

_____

_____

_____

_____

_____

_____

_____

_____

Chapter 2: Beauty for Ashes

To provide for those who grieve to bestow on them a crown of beauty instead of ashes." Isaiah 61:3

The feeling of wanting to be loved and accepted stemmed from that hole in my heart of being abandoned by my biological father and not feeling worthy. I struggled with low self-esteem and accepting who I was. I always felt different because of how much different I looked from my other family members. Additionally, never felt like I fit in with any ethnic or racial group. I was bullied in middle school about the way I looked and struggled with being confident in myself. As I would get older, that feeling didn't go away, and instead, I became more dependent on being validated by what a man would say or think about me. I ended up getting into relationships that were verbally and physically abusive and where I needed to feel needed; I found myself being attracted to men who were broken themselves. I spent years trying to fix a broken man into being the man I needed him to be for me as a broken woman. I ended up getting pregnant at 18 years old, and I remember when I found out how alone I felt and how disappointed my mother would be. I ended up having a miscarriage, and my mother flew from North Carolina to be by my side as I had a Dilation and curettage (D&C) surgery. I was depressed, sad, and cried all the time. It took me several weeks just to get back to myself. I had no idea how to fix myself because I poured all my energy and love into someone who didn't love me back. In Isaiah 61:3, the bible says, *"God will give you beauty for your ashes."* There were times where I felt like God had forgotten me and that the pain and abuse would never go away. As hard as it was to go through the constant name-calling and physical abuse, God had his hand on me and never left my side. I was reminded of this every time I came out alive of one of my abuser's erratic behaviors. God gave me beauty for my ashes, and no matter what situation I was in, He allowed me to live and see that there was purpose in my pain even if I couldn't see it.

What have you been so ashamed of?

Chapter 3: Just Let Me Die

I was 16 years old when I was involved in teen dating violence. It would take me a couple of years later when I realized what I had gone through because there wasn't anyone telling me the signs to look for. My parents had allowed me to start dating, and I had met this guy at my high school; I was a junior, and he was a senior. He was very charming, nice and showed interest in me. I was so happy that someone a little older than me liked me so much. The relationship started great, and my emotions were on cloud nine, but after a few months, things began to change. He became verbally abusive and controlling. I eventually ended the relationship before going to college, and I had realized that I had never dealt with the pain from that relationship. I got into another relationship a year later, and I started to see similar signs from the past relationship with the verbal abuse and controlling behavior. Still, this time it was different because it would also become physical. I was already so broken that I looked past the behavior and wanted to fix the problem, and thought that I could ultimately fix him. I realized that no matter how hard I try to fix the situation, you can't fix a broken man or woman. The slightest thing could set him off, and he was constantly paranoid about everything; I felt like I was constantly on trial... I was literally blinded by the exterior that I couldn't see that this wasn't right. I had become so conditioned to

The name-calling that after a while, I didn't even recognize that it was happening and just became numb to it. One of the awakening moments that I remember in the abuse was when the name-calling became my death sentence, and after he became enraged and angry because of a disagreement we had, he stated, "I should just let you die." As hard as that was, I was already so numb that I just could not feel any emotions. I saw my face on the news, and I had been stabbed to death in a domestic violence dispute. I woke up crying, sweating, and my heart racing. I knew at that moment that I had to make a change for myself and children. I can remember having a conversation with my mom and her telling me that if a man makes you cry more than he makes you smile, then it's time to reevaluate the relationship and walk away.

I was at my lowest point, depressed, isolated and weak. I had been going through this trauma for seven years. No one knew my pain, the tears I cried at night, the hospital visits I checked myself into to avoid the abuse, the marks around my neck and scarfs I would wear in the summer to cover up the choking marks around my neck, the make-up I wore to cover up my black eyes and the stories I would make up to people about my wounds. For years, I had to be careful of what I said and how I said it, and what I did to avoid verbal and physical abuse. I had even contemplated taking my own life because I was tired of the scars externally and internally. My girls were my push that I needed, and seeing them made me realize that I had to break the generational cycle and it had to stop with me.

They deserved better, and so did I. My life mattered and being able to watch my girls grow mattered to me. My heart was broken, and I didn't know how to repair it. I didn't know what to do, but I knew that my girls needed me, and that was enough to let go and start healing. I lived with the guilt that I had failed my mother, who had only wanted me to finish college because it was something that she could not do. I felt that I owed her that much to finish my Bachelor's no matter what it took to do it. I wanted a better life for my children.

What's your story?

_____

_____

_____

_____

_____

_____

_____

_____

_____

_____

_____

_____

_____

_____

What guilt have you held on to?

_____

_____

_____

_____

_____

_____

_____

_____

_____

_____

_____

_____

What things in your life made you feel like you couldn't go anymore?

Chapter 4: Isolation

I went through a dark period where I completely isolated myself from my family and friends close to me. My mother and I had always been close, but I found myself so broken and damaged that I couldn't stand to tell her what I had been going through. My mother was not on board with me leaving to go to college far away, but she knew she had to let me go to find my way. I found a man who physically abused me, belittled me, and emotionally left me broken. I didn't know how to tell my mother that her once strong, fearless, and brave girl was scared and weak. The truth is, I didn't know how to face reality, and I hated the woman I had become. I would hide my scars with make-up, make excuses for his behavior, and at times even blame myself for the abuse. I questioned my worth and even my decisions. I knew this wasn't me, and I searched for a long time to find that girl my family once knew, fearless, bold, and strong. In this isolation period, I couldn't find her. I was physically present but mentally and emotionally absent.

My family had no idea as to what I was going through. I would hide behind my smile, and I would try my hardest to be happy, but deep down, I was angry, scared, and in a lot of pain. When those moments of isolation became too much, I would grab a journal and write out my feelings and thoughts. Writing provided me the opportunity to connect within myself and to be free with my thoughts, words, and emotions. It gave me a sense of peace and hope. Isolating myself did not fix my problems; it only covered up what the real issues were and allowed me to mask my pain for a temporary feeling. My wounds of hurt, shame, and anger were still there until I was able to confront it and free myself so that I could begin to heal. I had to find a way not to be ashamed and to stop blaming myself. Did it come easy? No... but was it worth it? Yes! I am here today as a testament that Faith brought me through but believing is what keeps me Free!!

Recall a moment where you isolated yourself? How did it make you feel, and what was going through your mind?

_____

_____

_____

_____

_____

_____

_____

_____

_____

_____

_____

_____

Chapter 5: Victim to Victorious

I was 22 years old when I was diagnosed with a rare disease called Gestational Trophoblastic Disease. I found out shortly after I had miscarried and had gone through a Dilation and Curettage (D&C) when I got the call from my doctor's office that something was wrong and that I would have to undergo chemotherapy to help reduce the risk of it spreading; I had stage 1 where the tumor was in my uterus. I had been estranged from most of my family because of the abuse and isolation. This completely broke me in ways I didn't know I could actually feel. The pain that I felt with every chemotherapy visit was one that I wouldn't wish on anyone to deal with. I had to do it alone, and as scary as it was, I learned so much about myself through that process. I remember one of my Chemotherapy visits, and there was an older lady that was also getting her Chemo treatment. We started conversing about how long she has been battling cancer, and she stated that she was my age when she was first diagnosed. She had so much confidence and faith that she would beat it again. I remember asking her how she keeps it together emotionally with having cancer so many times. Her response to me was, "I am going to beat this and not let it beat me." I had isolated myself from my family and friends, and no one knew that I was carrying this pain and battling cancer. I did not know how to confront my pain or even understand how to fight through it. Chemotherapy was a fight for my life, and I knew that I had to fight this and not let it beat me, but I just did not know how to? I had to fight the good fight and remember God's purpose for my life. I had to get in front of this fight and remind myself that if God has been bringing me through the abuse, He will bring me through this too!

What things have you had to fight for in your life?

Chapter 6: The Shift

Taking the step to walk away was not easy but understanding that my life mattered gave me enough reason to do so. . I had to put my big girl panties on and remind myself that I am worthy of so much more. I graduated from the University of North Texas in May 2017. It took me almost seven years to get my Bachelor's degree, but I was determined to get my degree and walk across the stage. It didn't come easy and what I endured was hard. I worked two full-time jobs and traveled 1 hour to school for my night classes, taking my daughters with me to class because I didn't have anyone else to help me. I wouldn't get home until 11:00 p.m and would get my girls to bed and get up and do it all over again at 6:00 a.m. I couldn't give up, and I knew that my girls depended on me, and so to have them watch me walk across the stage with my diploma in hand was the best feeling ever, one of my proudest moments. I felt like I had failed my family because of my choices, but when I received my diploma, I knew that my life had meaning and purpose in my pain. My mess had a message, and all the tests I had been through were worth it. To be able to share my testimony in how God brought me through this. I just needed to start healing and transforming my mind from victim to victorious. As much pain, I had endured for years from the physical and verbal abuse to being diagnosed with cancer at the age of twenty-two. My mind had to shift to begin to see not my problems but my purpose. The shift for me happened when I found hope within my pain that things could be better, but I had to make the first move by completely letting go and stop trying to fight a battle that God already won on my behalf. Romans 5:3-5. *"We can rejoice when we run into problems and trials too, for we know that they help us develop endurance."*

What was the shift in your life?

What are some of your greatest accomplishments?

Chapter 7: Fired Up

After making the shift, I thought I had found my purpose. I had moved back home and was surrounded by my family and loved ones, who at one point during my abuse, I was isolated from. I was happy externally, but internally I was still struggling with my pain. I had not completely dealt with the pain and was masking it day by day. I was searching for happiness, but nothing seemed to make me happy truly. From the outside looking in, I was happy, but on the inside, I felt trapped and in bondage. I had a lot of trauma that would keep me up at night from the abuse and feeling like I failed my children. I had to stop avoiding the pain and start acknowledging it and give myself permission to work through it in my time.

Just when I thought things couldn't get any worse, my oldest daughter, who was four years old, began waking up in the middle of the night with painful headaches; this continued for several weeks. She would cry and scream because of the pain. I had mentioned it to her pediatrician and ophthalmologist, who thought it was related to her prior eye surgeries from being diagnosed at 6 months with Duane Syndrome, which is an eye movement disorder, where she had to have multiple eye surgeries. I kept a close eye on it, but it seemed to be getting worse and worse as the weeks went on. On January 12, 2017, I had to rush my daughter to Children's Hospital of King's Daughter urgent care because she had not been feeling well at school and had thrown up in the car. The doctor explained to me that her blood pressure was very high and that she had a very high fever. . We were rushed by ambulance to the main Children's Hospital where she was hooked up to machines and monitors in ICU and underwent multiple tests and scans. I remember losing my mind, I called my mother, who was on her way, but I felt so helpless and scared. I had so many things going through my mind, and none of it made sense but what I was not prepared for was what the doctors said. After several hours of waiting and holding my daughter's tiny hands as she slept and the monitors beeping and the fluids going through her veins, I hear a knock at the door, and four people walked into the room, tears were flowing from my face, and one of the doctors asked if I was the mother; I answered yes, and he asked if I could step outside to talk to his team. The neurosurgeon explained to me that after reviewing my daughter's MRI scans, they have determined that she has a Cavernous Malformation which is a collection of small blood vessels (capillaries) in the central nervous system that is enlarged and irregular in structure. In CCM, the capillaries' walls are thinner than normal, less elastic, and are likely to leak. My daughter's blood vessels had a hemorrhage, which led to the swelling in her brain. She was placed on blood pressure medication for a few months and steroids to reduce the swelling in her brain. After a long seven months of waiting for her swelling to decrease in her brain, hospital visits, MRI scans, and frequent visits to her Neurosurgeon at Georgetown University Hospital, she had the Cavernous Malformation removed on August 9, 2018.

For almost a year, I watched my daughter's strength and resilience in how she would pray and ask God to heal her and how she would tenderly remind me that she will be okay. I would cry and ask God, "Why her?" But what I couldn't see in those moments was God's plan and purpose. I remember praying and getting angry at God that this was happening to my baby – she had already been through so much trauma that this did not seem fair. I felt like I had failed my daughter, and I just wanted to take the pain away and carry it for her, but God's word reminded me in John 16:20 ***"Very truly I tell you, you will weep and mourn while the world rejoices. You will grieve, but your grief will turn to joy."***

I had to put my total and complete faith in God in that the same way He brought me through my own battle with cancer and with the abuse believing that He will cover and protect my daughter. This will be her testimony and message – how she, too, overcame something traumatic and God healed her too. My weeping may endure for the night, but my joy will come soon. I had to stop trying to carry this weight and give it back to God. I had to stop trying to fight a battle that God had already won. I had to give myself permission that it's okay not to be okay. Often in our healing process, we feel like we have to live up to a certain standard or do things by how others want us to react and feel. There were some days where I didn't want to get out of bed; I would have triggers and flashbacks of the traumatic experiences. My headspace at times was all over the place, and I couldn't understand how on the outside I was so happy and fired up with life, but on the inside, I was breaking, emotionally unstable, and unbalanced. What I came to recognize is that healing takes time. How much time? I don't know. I know that it has taken almost five years, and I am still working through it- but it's a push within myself that I work on daily. In Mark 5:34, *"He said to her, Daughter, your faith has healed you. Go in peace and be freed from your suffering."* I have suffered long enough, and now it's time to love myself and be at peace knowing I have done all that I can do, and when I can't do anymore, I will surrender my heart and mind to God, and He will heal. I will find refuge and comfort in knowing that He already has won the battle for me.

WHOLENESS

Wholeness does not mean perfection: it means embracing brokenness as an integral part of life. By: Parker J. Palmer

Chapter 8: The Healing Process: Healing in Time

When you heal, you permit yourself not to be stuck in an unpleasant feeling of hopelessness, shame, guilt, and fear. The feeling of not being able to let go because you have deep pain that is keeping you from living your fullest potential. The questions I asked myself many times in this process are, "How do I let go? How do I stop blaming myself for someone else's problems? How do I move forward without carrying the guilt and shame with me?" There are no clear answers because every healing journey is different, much like being injured in a sport or car accident, the impact may be the same, but the healing time will be different. I had to learn throughout my healing process to acknowledge it; once I acknowledged it, I could begin to heal. I had fears that acknowledging my pain would only make it worse for me to move forward mentally. I didn't want it to control me and keep me in bondage. The only way it can control you is if you let it! I realized that taking back control meant that I had to be intentional about speaking positive affirmations. I couldn't continue to blame myself for what happened. The past is a part of history, and I can either live in history or get ready for my future. Your past doesn't have to be your future. As a matter of fact, the only person who has control of that is YOU!

Healing in your own time is when you understand that there isn't a time limit to the healing process. The healing process isn't a quick fix that happens overnight but can take months and sometimes years. I've learned from this process that once you can heal, you will forgive and not just forgive yourself but forgiving the person that has hurt you. You can smile without faking it, and your glow will be authentic. I like to look at the healing process in three ways.

1. **Refinement** (Acknowledgment) taking the first step to making the change.

2. **Releasing-** Letting go of the pain, hurt, and toxins in your life

3. **Reconstructing-** In this stage, we don't want to go back to or repair what we were coming out of but really seek God through this healing journey and permit ourselves to be okay with not being okay. Ultimately becoming a better us!

What are your triggers in this healing process? Identify your pain and speak on it... naming it will allow you to heal from it and not allow your mind to be *revictimized* repeatedly. Take back your life and be in control to say that you will not just hide behind it but face it and challenge yourself to be strategic about your healing and what that pain looks like. *Acknowledging* it doesn't mean that you are a victim still, but it means you are facing your problem and not allowing it to control your mind or emotions. Lastly, and probably the most important piece of the healing process is to be *STILL.* The act of stillness is when you can turn off your mind from thinking and doing. In stillness, you are letting go of what runs in your mind and not reacting to anything that is going on around you. Being **STILL** comes with some challenges because even when I am asleep, my mind constantly thinks about everything. I can't seem to turn it off. For me to begin to heal, my therapist suggested that I be still in the moment. I remember thinking to myself, "How in the world do I do that?" Perhaps she must not know me very well or didn't listen to me in what I am saying to her so that I can't turn off my mind from thinking. It wasn't until I really started to think about what she was saying and started to get into my healing process where I was able to completely remove myself from all the noise around me and sit in a quiet, dark space where I would close my eyes and focus on my breathing, it was in that moment where my mind left my body, and I was able to be **STILL.** The peace that evoked my body was transformational. I let go of my fears, worries, doubts, anger, and regrets and just focused on my peace and me. I used to take these moments for granted for just being **STILL**. When you find it, you find your happy place. You get to escape for a moment and Be Free! Bob Marley once said, "None but ourselves can free our minds." This means that we are the only ones that can truly free ourselves from what we think and feel. No one else can do that but You! My favorite bible verse is Psalms 46:10 *"Be Still and know I am God..."* -

Affirmations

I cannot change what has happened in my past, but I change how I move forward into my future

I am on my way to healing

I am healing in my own time

I am a little bent, but I am not broken

Chapter 9: Redefining Self-Love

Throughout the healing process, defining self-love was something that I did not know how to define honestly. It was a word that was hard for me to think about because I never thought about what I loved about myself and, most importantly, how to love myself. When you uncover the word self-love, you begin to understand that loving who you are can accept who you were and who you are. When you redefine self-love, you can do the following: Accepting your mistakes – not as failures but as an area for growth. You're constantly changing and growing from who you once were into who you are today and who you inspire to be.

I've unlocked **12 steps to take to redefine self-love:**

1. Make Mistakes

This is powerful because, as people, we don't want to fail at things, and small failures can pull us down to the point of wanting to give up. Don't throw in the towel; instead, embrace your mistakes and welcome them as a part of growth to level up and become a better version of yourself.

2. Say Goodbye to Toxins

Toxic things or people are not something that you want to keep around. Not only is it bad for us physically but also mentally and emotionally! It leaves us broken, drained and exhausted. Toxic things create an emptiness in your heart and pull the energy from your soul. Take back the control and let go of the negative energy that brings you down to preserve the positive energy that you deserve. This might mean walking away from some people in your life to protect your energy. Don't be afraid to do this; it's not selfish but self-love. It's freedom, and it's liberating; even though it's painful, it's necessary to grow into a better version of yourself and redefine self-love.

3. Let go of your Fears

Process what is keeping you up and what is bringing you down. Fear is a silent energy sucker and can lead you into a dark path of depression. Interrogating and evaluating your fears helps you to gain clarity and unmask issues in your life that were causing you anxiety.

4. Process Every Decision

We so often doubt ourselves and our ability to do what's right, when most of the time we do know in our hearts what's best. Remember that your feelings are valid. You're not losing touch with reality. You know yourself better than anyone else. So, be your best advocate!

5. Investing Yourself

The best version of yourself is YOU! What is stopping you from seizing the moment to reach your dreams, goals and to walk in your purpose? The only thing that stops you from achieving what you want is YOU? Don't block or stop what

God's plan is for your life. Sometimes we can get in our own way because of self-doubt, timing, and a well of emotions. Understand that timing will never ever be perfect for taking a step towards your self-purpose. Drive your fear and negative thoughts out and focus on what you truly want and what happiness looks like for you.

6. Self- Purpose

Even if you don't know your purpose, focus on what drives you into becoming a better you. Walk like you have a purpose, talk like you have a purpose, love like you have a purpose, believe like you have a purpose, and get up every day putting yourself first in that your purpose is to live the life that you believe and dream of living. Write out what you want and make it plain and simple to see to help visually see your goals and to make what's in your head make sense with your reality vs. fantasy.

7. Identifying Joyful Pain

Being in tune with your pain will help you to heal. It's when we ignore it that will keep us in a state of uncertainty and fear. Lean into your pain so that you can enjoy your joy, peace, and full happiness. Joy and pain are emotions that help you understand yourself better, and realize that you're not stuck in a feeling of self-doubt and uncertainty.

8. Be Courageous

Be Bold! Boldness is like a muscle; the more you exercise, the more it grows. Don't wait for someone to validate you but instead speak to your inner self to know your worth and take action for what you inspire to become.

9. Be intentionally Kind to yourself

Celebrate YOURSELF! When we go through things a lot of times, we lose focus on the little things that keep us motivated, and when we are intentional about self-love and being able to celebrate our glows and growth, it shows that we are healing in the right direction. You've come through too much not to celebrate and enjoy loving you – not just on your birthday, but every day.

10. Block out the negative voices

To be the best You! ...You have to block out negative voices and energy that tries to bring you down. This is easier said than done, but it doesn't mean that it can't be done. It just means you have to be intentional to focus on your healing and grows and glows through the healing process. No one said that it will be easy, but you will get through it. My grandmother used to say, "The race is not for the swift but for those who endure it." Endure for a season so that you can live your best life for the rest of your life.

11. Love the skin you're in

Be comfortable with not being comfortable. Life is about change, and if we haven't learned anything about life and ourselves, we have to be okay with where we are and that we are in the healing process. Some days will be bad, and some days will be good, but through every day, you are accepting and exercising patience with yourself.

12. Be Free

Focus on what you can control and let go of what you can't control. Free your mind from negativity and be blissful in freedom!

Focus on your journey to heal and shift your energy to love who you are from the inside and out. If you follow these steps, you will free yourself and be on your way to a better YOU!

Healing in time gives you the control to not erase your past but to forgive for your future- Sierrah Chavis

Chapter 10: Burn the Burden

For seven years, I didn't have my own voice. I had to walk on eggshells and never knew what to say or how to say it because I was afraid of how my abuser would react and its repercussions. So many times, I would just be silenced. So I found my peace by writing. The writing was my escape from the world. I was able to get all my anger and feelings on paper without anyone knowing. Although I was writing, my pain was still there, and the burden seemed to get bigger. I had to be comfortable with being uncomfortable. Something inside me had to break. In my healing journey, I've learned that negative energy will cause you to develop the mindset of defeat. You think that no one understands what you've been through, so you feel alone in your thoughts and feelings. I began to isolate myself from my family and friends because the burden was too big for me to understand at times. Self-doubt will lead you through a path of self-destruction and depression. I had to get into a mindset that I will not allow my thoughts to run my life and dictate my every move. I had to begin to ask myself what kind of life do I want to live? And what type of happiness do I want to have? Asking myself these questions and then writing them down allowed me to think more positively and see my life differently. Happiness is defined differently by different people. If you ask one person how they define happiness, it may be completely different than another person, but both people will be happy, right? When you ask yourself what defines your happiness, it will help you think and feel better about yourself and keep your mind from being burdened with negative thoughts and energy that disrupt your peace. Don't be a prisoner in your own mind; take back your peace! Be intentional about being happy and block the negative energy that your mind wants to travel to.

Chapter 11: Purpose in your Pain

My pain came from the physical and verbal abuse, battling cancer and watching my daughter go through a traumatic illness. It was hard to talk about the things that had caused me so much pain. I couldn't see that the pain I was feeling in those moments of uncertainty prepared me for my ultimate purpose. Often, we hear this but are not sure how it applies to us, not just physically but emotionally, that we often can't see our purpose when dealing with so much pain. We feel like our pain is too deep to even have a purpose. It's not just a metaphor but a mindset to change the way you think by giving yourself permission to live to your potential. My pain gave me strength that I didn't know I had before. One of my favorite scriptures is Philippians 4:13 ***"I can do all things through Christ who strengthens me."*** Even if you don't believe it, keep saying it because eventually, your words will catch up with your heart and mind - you will walk differently, talk differently, and see the world around you differently. It has to start with you! Don't forget your pain but heal from it so that you can find purpose in what you've been through, and drop gems to help others understand their purpose too. Your pain does not define you, but it can heal you and push you to excel, and build you up to become the best version of yourself. My pain provided me the courage to speak to other women about domestic violence and teen dating violence; to empower women to live their best lives and to be able to continue to encourage me at the same time.

Chapter 12: Unleash your Purpose

When I stopped trying to avoid my pain, I could then accept myself and stop burdening my mind with blame. You can miss your purpose by allowing yourself to avoid the painful stuff and by trying to find something to protect yourself from it. The pain did not destroy me, but it revealed who I was. Imagine looking in the mirror and seeing your reflection looking back at you. What do you see? Are you proud of who is looking back at you? I had to ask myself these difficult questions. The more painful things I went through, the more I discovered about myself and my own strengths. We must interpret our pain through the lens of God's purpose for us. My purpose was hiding behind my pain, and until I was able to see that there was purpose in my pain, it would continue to remain painful. Did you ever stop and wonder why you experience pain? Have you ever assessed your pain to find out the purpose of it? If everything works for your good, you must understand pain does as well, as painful as that may be. Two critical decisions must be made in the moment of Pain:

1. The first is to determine what to do in your Pain
2. Secondly, what to do with your Pain

The first has to do with **You,** while the second has to do with **Others**. Pain is inevitable, but suffering is optional. You can lie around in your pain, or you can turn it around and actually choose to use it for your good. What will be your choice?

Don't be afraid of your scars, for those scars become the lighthouse for others to see that there is also purpose in their pain. Your messes will become your message, and your trials will become your triumph! Your adversity will become your advancement! Your frustration will become your fuel, and your scars will become your star! You will light this world on fire with your smile; you will say, "Thank God I don't look like what I've been through." If they only knew the tears you cried at night, the sleepless nights you had because you stayed up thinking and contemplating things in your head. In the moments you feel unworthy and not beautiful, I am here to tell you that you are more than enough! you are a survivor, you are strong and your voice matters. Don't let your pain overshadow your potential in being something so Amazing. Your pain has purpose. Get up Girl! The world needs you.

Chapter 13: Having a Winners Attitude

When you take the approach that you have already won the battle despite the circumstances, you are positioning yourself in having a winner's attitude towards your pain. You are converting your "bitterness into betterness," "misery into ministry," and "adversity into advancement." You believe that there is a light at the end of the tunnel. I felt many times broken down and defeated because of all the pain I had endured for so long. I couldn't seem to look past the pain and had a mindset that I had already lost. What I didn't realize was that God was moving on my behalf the entire time and that even though I felt like I had failed, God had already won the battle for me. I just needed to trust him through the process. It's when I truly understood my message that I was able to overcome my pain. I had to ask myself these questions...

"How could the story of my pain offer hope to somebody else who needs to hear my story?"

How has my pain changed my attitude toward others who are suffering?

What can I create or produce that would be a resource of hope for others?

How is my pain prompting me to make changes in how I live my life?

How is my pain prompting me to make my remaining days matter?

What is God saying to me in my pain?

Chapter 14: Growing and Glowing

I am growing everyday and learning something new about myself. That saying, "Thank God I don't look like what I've been through," means a lot. What I've been through in my life caused me to be comfortable with masking my pain and as I became uncomfortable with revealing the mask I was only then able to embrace it as an opportunity to grow and glow in areas that I didn't think I had the strength to do.There are still certain parts of me that are healing, but I understand my worth and have set my expectations and standards for what I will and will not accept. My heart is full and in a place of receiving love. I have not always felt like this, but when I focused on loving myself and turning my pain into my purpose, I could love and be loved. My hopelessness turned into wholeness because I was no longer a prisoner of war trapped and held back from believing that no one, including myself, could love or be worthy enough to be loved. My glow is different; it is authentic and genuine; I don't have to fake it till I make it. I am a work in progress, and every day I work on becoming a better version of myself. When I moved out my own way and allowed God to move in my life, I saw a change in how I could live my best life. As a mother of three beautiful girls, I want them to see the strength and also see that you don't have to look like what you've been through. I decided to break those generational barriers and show my girls that love doesn't and shouldn't hurt. I am raising them to have self-love and to know their worth every day. Their **Glow** will be different because my **Growth** is transformational. The generational curse stopped with me.

Chapter 15: Hopelessness to Wholeness

When I came home, I realized that the person I was 13 years ago was broken. I had stopped laughing, I had stopped smiling, and I had lost my voice. I had hidden behind my smile because deep down, I was hurting. I needed to find that young, bold, brave, courageous smile again; That didn't have to hide any longer or be afraid to use her voice out of fear of what would happen if she did. In finding me, I found self-love. I could not think about giving myself to anyone else until I could love myself again and take back what was taken from me. I had to own my mistakes, forgive and allow myself to be free. At the beginning of my healing process, it was hard to process the idea of loving someone again. I had given so much of myself and energy to someone who left me feeling empty and broken. I didn't feel worthy of having someone love me and accept me for who I was and what I came with, two children and a lot of painful scars and memories. The thought of finding someone to love me left me feeling hopeless and in fear that I would never find love again, and those things only happen in movies. When I stopped trying to play out the negative scenarios in my mind and started to accept my journey in the   healing process, which included learning to love myself first, I was able to turn my *Hopelessness into Wholeness.* I didn't feel broken or damaged, I felt complete and my heart was unified. In feeling *whole,* I had vowed to God that I would trust Him and seek Him first. My *wholeness* was not measured by someone else's love for me but by the love that I gave to myself, first.

Chapter 16: The Good Fight

Fantasia Barrino said it best in her song, "Sometimes You have to Lose to Win Again!" I realized that the things that I've been through were not to harm or hurt me, although I felt like it, but to mentally and emotionally prepare me to break down generational cycles, help others work through their pain, and live a life of Freedom and Peace. I found hope in knowing that when I trust God through the process, He will show up and show out on my behalf! It's not easy to let go because that means you have allowed yourself to receive help for a pain you were trying to escape. The Good Fight I call life is about understanding that it will give you some lemons, and you can choose to either collect the lemons or make lemonade and celebrate your freedom! Stay in the Good Fight and remember that "healing is a process that takes time to grow; you will have to grow into your healing!" Grow and Glow, and don't stop the Good Fight of life; instead, embrace it with open arms that you will not have to cry the same tears but that God will show up for the battle-ready to fight for you. However, you first have to leave all your worries, fears, and anxiety in the past and focus on healing from your pain. After all that I have been through, my prayers have been answered, my faith is renewed. Don't get it twisted, I am still on my healing journey but my smile is bigger, my voice is louder, my heart is open, and my mind is clear and in peace. I walk in confidence and without regrets. I surrender to God my worries, fears, anxiety, pain, tears, doubts and become completely mentally and emotionally bare with God. In Deuteronomy 32:35, *"It is mine to avenge; I will repay. In due time their foot will slip; their day of disaster is near, and their doom rushes upon them."* What you do to one of God's children, you do unto Him. I didn't have to consume myself with revenge or payback because God showed up for the battle on my behalf and gave me beauty for my ashes. My story is ironically similar to the butterfly story. A caterpillar had been stuck in his cocoon, struggling to find a hole to push itself out, and after a long time of suffering, this caterpillar was able to find the hole and break free, spreading its wings and flying away. I was lost, broken, and trapped in pain, but when I finally found myself and gave myself back to God, I was only then able to be free, and it was time to spread my wings and turn my suffrage into salvation.

HOPELESSNESS TO WHOLENESS REFLECTION JOURNAL

Reflection is key when you are healing. I did a lot of soul searching, meditation and reflection by keeping a journal. It allowed me to find balanced arms.

I can start my healing process by............

What generational cycles are you breaking?

I am going to let go of ....

What or Who is your safe place? (to talk, vent, and to turn to for help)

List ways you can protect your energy.

Name 5 things that you love about yourself.

What are your fears?

What are your struggles?

_____

_____

_____

_____

_____

_____

_____

_____

_____

_____

_____

_____

_____

Do you know what your purpose is? Please explain your answer. If your answer is No, please explain why you think you don't know and what's holding you back from knowing your purpose?

What are your dreams, hopes, and goals for yourself (right now)?

What are your flaws?

What are your negative thoughts? (think about the things you tell yourself)

What keeps you up at night?

Define what happiness means to you.

What or Who motivates or pushes you?

If you could create a better version of yourself, what would that person look like? (Think beyond the physical)

Create your own affirmations (say them daily and post them where you spend most of your time). I like to post mine on my laptop as a reminder when I am working.

Healing poem

Dance, dance, dance!

For your soul and mind are free.

Your light shines bright like the sun beaming on a hot day.

You have lived a rough life, and it hasn't always been easy, but you are soaring like an eagle.

Your future awaits you, and it's bigger than you think.

The time is now to love who you are!

Forgive yourself for your past does not define you.

Find purpose in your pain and allow yourself to heal.

Give yourself a chance to love, hope, dream, and be free.

Cry no more sorrows and feel no more pain, for the joy that surrounds you is bigger than you can imagine

Turn your hopelessness into wholeness.

For your healing begins when you decide to live!

Written By: Sierrah Chavis

Made in the USA
Middletown, DE
26 August 2021